A Book of Common Rituals

Also by
Brian Clements

Poetry
not meant for you   Dear Love (Mudlark 49, 2012)
In Review (Red Glass Books, 2012)
Jargon (Quale Press, 2010)
And How to End It (Quale Press, 2008)
Disappointed Psalms (Meritage Press, 2008)
Use Cases (Mudlark 28, 2005)
Essays Against Ruin (Texas Review Press, 1997)
Flesh and Wood (Mbira Press, 1992)

Editor
An Introduction to the Prose Poem, with Jamey Dunham
(Firewheel Editions, 2009)

A Book of Common Rituals

Brian Clements

A ClearSound book from QUALE PRESS

Copyright © 2014 by Brian Clements

Cover art by Thomas Nackid

ISBN: 978-1-935835-13-4 trade paperback edition

LCCN: 2014950164

Quale Press
www.quale.com

Contents

Morning Rituals

    Ritual for Beginning · 2
    Ritual for Speaking · 6
    Coffee Ritual · 8
    Sky Ritual · 12
    Requiem Ritual · 14
    Santorini Ritual · 16
    Object Ritual · 18
    Ritual for Speaking II · 20

Afternoon Rituals

    Business Ritual · 24
    Office Work Ritual · 28
    Outdoor Work Ritual · 30
    Air Ritual · 32
    Boat Ritual · 34
    Ritual for Doing · 38
    Tree Ritual · 42
    Ritual for Eating · 44

Evening Rituals

    Negotiation Ritual · 48

    Blood Ritual · 50

    Subatomic Particle Ritual · 52

    Ritual With No Name · 54

    Tree Ritual II · 56

    Smoking Ritual · 58

    Searchlight Ritual · 60

    Numbers Ritual · 62

    Notes & Sources · 65

Morning Rituals

First Morning Ritual

Ritual for Beginning

Assemble a congregation. The congregants may come from your workplace, from the street, from a store. You may assemble them in any room. Even though they ask, it is not necessary to explain to them the reason for their congregation. You may not, however, lie.

Draw a line on the floor that extends from one end of the room to the other. Beyond the walls, this line extends indefinitely. If the line crosses itself, there is no need to continue.

Given that the line does not cross itself, stand on the side of the line opposite the congregation. Greet them.

[Behind you, the congregation notes the arrival of things that happened moments ago: a child ran across the street; a siren shifted past into the lower register; a cloud passed in front of the sun and dimmed the window.]

Pull the drapes or close the blinds. Shut off the light.

Light a small flame in your palm.

Carry the flame to the line.

Remove one man and one woman from the congregation. They must both be at least twelve years your elder.

Extinguish the flame and lie down on the line. Invite the man and woman to bisect you from crown to crotch with the ash from your palm along the axis of the line.

"Members of a congregation may assume that they hold common religious beliefs, but it is religious ritual that creates and sustains continued fellowship," says Dr. Daniel B. Lee assistant professor of sociology at Penn State's DuBois Campus.

"This is a key point for understanding the social structure of religious communities and the relationship between ritual and belief," Lee notes. "While an individual may sincerely hold religious beliefs, a group does not have a common mind and cannot hold any belief. Faith becomes socially relevant through action. Until there is action, religion is socially meaningless."

Admit there are no beginnings. That this began long ago.

You may now do one of two things:

    a. Divide yourself into two equal halves
    b. Just lie there and pay attention

Second Morning Ritual

Ritual for Speaking

At your leisure, browse one of the following:

    a. A library
    b. The WWW
    c. Facebook
    d. Cable/satellite TV

When you tire of browsing, walk alone for a mile in the direction of nothing.

Avoid speaking.

After at least one mile, walk back in the direction you came. Visualize the open space behind you.

Take the first song that comes to mind and put it in the open space. Follow the song into the open space. When you are completely inside, wait.

Who has the song in the open space become?

Speak to her.

Riding the other day along a track,
thinking of the journey I disliked,
I found Amor in the middle of the way
in the simple dress of a traveller.
In his countenance, wretched, he seemed to me
as if he had lost a ruler-ship:
and he came sighing thoughtfully
not seeing anyone, with head bowed low.
When he saw me he called me by name,
and said: 'I come from a distant place
from where your heart was according to my
    wish:
and bring it back to serve new pleasures.'
Then I took from him so great a part
that he vanished, and I did not see how.

    So, my imagination beginning to wander, I came to a place not knowing where I was: and it seemed to me I saw women, weeping, with dishevelled hair, going through the street, in extreme sadness: and the sun seemed to me to be darkened, so that the stars showed themselves of a colour such that I judged they were weeping: and it seemed to me that birds flying in the air fell dead, and there were massive tremors.

Third Morning Ritual

Coffee Ritual

Insert two fingers into a beehive. Lick one of them, then pack them both with dirt. Wipe off the whole mess into an empty coffee can.

Insert a hickory stick into a fire ant colony. Plunge it deep and grind. Grind the little fuckers some more. Remove the stick and kick the mound into the wind. Scrape whatever clings to the hickory stick into the coffee can.

Insert the hickory stick into a crawdad hole. If he grabs on, pull him out and put him in a plastic bag. Scrape the mud off the stick into the coffee can and drop in a tablespoon of wet coffee grounds.

Bait a trout hook with red salmon egg. Fish until you catch a speckled trout.

After dusk, put some water on to boil in the coffee pot.

Take a flashlight and the plastic bag to the river. Let the crawdad go. Watch where he runs. Catch a dozen more.

Drop the crawdads in the coffee pot. Dump in a bunch of salt.

Wrap the trout in foil and cook him in the coals.

Eat the crawdads, then the trout.

Throw the shells, fins, skin, and skeleton into the coffee can. Pour a cup of salt water from the coffee pot into the can.

One early use for coffee would have little appeal today. The Galla tribe from Ethiopia used coffee, but not as a drink. They would wrap the beans in animal fat as their only source of nutrition while on raiding parties.

> **Did You Know?**
>
> The heavy tea tax imposed on the colonies in 1773, which caused the "Boston Tea Party," resulted in America switching from tea to coffee. Drinking coffee was an expression of freedom.

Dump the coffee pot and wash it in the river. Put on a pot of coffee to boil.

Drink coffee.

Drop a nightcrawler into the coffee can.

In the morning, bury the can until ready for coffee again.

Fourth Morning Ritual

Sky Ritual

For four days, collect in a pail all of the liquids that touch your skin: rain, milk, spit, semen, windex. . .

On the fifth day, skim the layer of scum from the top of the pail. Dry it in the sun; you will get a light meerschaum, the lightest residue of your body's absence, light as frozen smoke.

Clip your twenty nails to the cuticle. If you bleed, drip some of the blood into your residue. Arrange the nails around your residue in a circle.

Near this arrangement, construct out of grass and sticks a small hut the size of a fist.

Rake an inch-deep trench past the hut and allow water to trickle into the trench.

Sprinkle your residue with the waters of the trickling river. Mash the wet residue, the nails, the grass, and the sticks into a ball and whisper over it the names of its past selves.

Place the ball into a sling and shoot it into the sky.

I have stated that the most probable hypothesis to account for the reappearance of very ancient characters, is—that there is a *tendency* in the young of each successive generation to produce the long-lost character, and that this tendency, from unknown causes, sometimes prevails. And we have just seen that in several species of the horse genus the stripes are either plainer or appear more commonly in the young than in the old. Call the breeds of pigeons, some of which have bred true for centuries, species; and how exactly parallel is the case with that of the species of the horse genus! For myself, I venture confidently to look back thousands on thousands of generations, and I see an animal striped like a zebra, but perhaps otherwise very differently constructed, the common parent of our domestic horse (whether or not it be descended from one or more wild stocks), of the ass, the hemionus, quagga, and zebra.

He who believes that each equine species was independently created, will, I presume, assert that each species has been created with a tendency to vary, both under nature and under domestication, in this particular manner, so as often to become striped like the other species of the genus; and that each has been created with a strong tendency, when crossed with species inhabiting distant quarters of the world, to produce hybrids resembling in their stripes, not their own parents, but other species of the genus. To admit this view, is, as it seems to me, to reject a real for an unreal, or at least for an unknown cause. It makes the works of God a mere mockery and deception; I would almost as soon believe, with the old and ignorant cosmogonists, that fossil shells had never lived, but had been created in stone so as to mock the shells living on the seashore.

· 13

FIFTH MORNING RITUAL

Requiem Ritual

Find an earthworm and praise the earthworm, for it is always there.

Open a book and praise the book, for it always speaks.

Turn on the television and praise the television, for it has another story.

Do not praise the rifle.

Find your pulse and take it to brunch. Buy it a Bellini.

Put on Mozart's *Requiem.* And then Chet Baker.

Find water in the air. Find water in the ground.

Find the earthworm.

For if you look at the aspect which changes, heaven and earth cannot last for one blink; but if you look at the aspect which is changeless, the worlds within and outside you are both inexhaustible, and what reasons have you to envy anything?

SIXTH MORNING RITUAL

Santorini Ritual

Take a boat to Santorini. Circle around the island and look skyward. Claim you are a pendulum hanging from the pupil of Athena's left eye.

Disembark. Avoid the donkeys. Ride to the peak of the island on the back of a moped. Pay the driver with two Atlantian dollars you made yourself. Walk out of town through a vineyard.

Eat a dusty green grape. Spit it out. Eat an olive. Spit out the pit. Build a tiny amphitheatre in the middle of the vineyard using nothing but bread crusts and cucumber rinds.

Walk to Monolithos. Take off your clothes and roll on the black glass beach. Chase a tourist with a mirror.

In front of the property of a native resident, try to catch a fish with your bare hands. When you fail, exhibit your belly as evidence of your hunting prowess.

Try to attract lovers in town by spreading your legs and sucking lemons in the street. Braid your hair like Bo Derek's. Show off the crude oil crusted between your toes.

After three days, make the whole island want you by pretending you are going to leave.

... I believe that these ancient maps do preserve such important ancient knowledge, and they are priceless evidence of advanced science in antiquity. But I do not interpret them as evidence of 'Atlantis'; I see them as yet more survivals of knowledge left by visiting extraterrestrials, who were able to map the Earth from space, and who were able to detect the true continental outline of Antarctica *through the ice* by orbiting space observations in the same way that we can do today.

SEVENTH MORNING RITUAL

Object Ritual

Collect the objects you will need for your day.

Be sure to include among them the telephone.

Place the objects into your pocket and walk to a public place.

Be sure to include among them the page, the flag, the stone.

Place the objects on a low wall along a sidewalk.

Be sure to include the wind, the glasses, the tongue, the dream.

Step back and listen to what they say.

Script for object monologues:

The Telephone
You are wrong about everything.

The Glasses
I lost your eyes.

The Page
What more can I say?

The Tongue
There is always more to say.

The Flag
Iron on the tongue.

The Flag
A dictionary of wind.

The Wind
A hallway in your dream.

The Dream
What you never said.

The Dream
What you never said.

The Telephone
Look out for the…

Eighth Morning Ritual

Ritual for Speaking II

Prepare for oration by staring out a window as though it were a mirror.

Meet your audience on the road.

Begin by humming a quiet chant designed to warm their affections.

Make no quotations and no reference to any other speaker.

If the audience loves you, sit down with them. If they fear you, sit down behind them and project before them the history of your coming to meet them.

Move closer. Close enough so that when you speak, it is not to speak, but to touch.

3

On, on I go, (open doors of time! open hospital doors!)
The crush'd head I dress, (poor crazed hand tear not the bandage away,)
The neck of the cavalry-man with the bullet through and through I examine,
Hard the breathing rattles, quite glazed already the eye, yet life struggles hard,
(Come sweet death! be persuaded O beautiful death!
In mercy come quickly.)

From the stump of the arm, the amputated hand,
I undo the clotted lint, remove the slough, wash off the matter and blood,
Back on his pillow the soldier bends with curv'd neck and side falling head,
His eyes are closed, his face is pale, he dares not look on the bloody stump,
And has not yet look'd on it.

I dress a wound in the side, deep, deep,
But a day or two more, for see the frame all wasted and sinking,
And the yellow-blue countenance see.

I dress the perforated shoulder, the foot with the bullet-wound,
Cleanse the one with a gnawing and putrid gangrene, so sickening, so offensive,
While the attendant stands behind aside me holding the tray and pail.

I am faithful, I do not give out,
The fractur'd thigh, the knee, the wound in the abdomen,
These and more I dress with impassive hand, (yet deep in my breast a fire, a burning
    flame.)

Afternoon Rituals

First Afternoon Ritual

Business Ritual

Travel to the office of a distant business partner. Greet him or her by holding one hand to your ear and waving the other hand in the air as though pointing to a satellite circling above.

Adjourn to a conference room and tape a sign to the door that says "Privates." Claim only to understand the languages of love and money, but respond in a different English dialect every time you are addressed.

Sit in chairs opposite each other. There should be no table between you. Place your hands in your laps and recite the Preamble to the Constitution of the United States of America.

For the next quarter of an hour, exchange memos regarding Middle East politics. For the next quarter of an hour, take turns closing your eyes while the other makes ugly faces. For the next quarter of an hour, pry into each other's briefcases. For the next quarter of an hour, watch traffic in the hallway, grading each passerby on the similarity of his or her walk to that of Winston Churchill.

Go to dinner and pull out paperwork that transfers rights to Hong Kong to each other. Shred the paper and drop it in your salad. Complain to the waiter. Admit to the *Maitre d'* that you have no idea how you got there or what it is you're supposed to be doing. Claim that you should be on an island off the coast of Argentina selling handhelds to fishermen.

There is nothing uniquely Western about colonialism. My native country of India, for example, was ruled by the British for more than two centuries, and many of my fellow Indians are still smarting about that. What they often forget, however, is that before the British came, the Indians had been invaded and conquered by the Persians, the Afghans, Alexander the Great, the Mongols, the Arabs, and the Turks. Depending on how you count, the British were preceded by at least six colonial powers that invaded and occupied India since ancient times. Indeed, ancient India was itself settled by the Aryan people, who came from the north and subjugated the dark-skinned indigenous people.

Those who identify colonialism and empire only with the West either have no sense of history or have forgotten about the Egyptian empire, the Persian empire, the Macedonian empire, the Islamic empire, the Mongol empire, the Chinese empire, and the Aztec and Inca empires in the Americas. Shouldn't the Arabs be paying reparations for their destruction of the Byzantine and Persian empires? Come to think of it, shouldn't the Byzantine and Persian people be paying reparations to the descendants of the people they subjugated? And while we're at it, shouldn't the Muslims reimburse the Spaniards for their 700-year rule?

Extent of Colonialism

(1939)

****	Great Britain	France	Belgium	Netherlands	Germany (1914)
Area in Square Miles	94,000	212,600	11,800	13,200	210,000
Population	45,500,100	42,000,000	8,300,000	8,500,000	67,500,000
Area of Colonies	13,100,000	4,300,000	940,000	790,000	1,100,000
Population of Colonies	470,000,000	65,000,000	13,000,000	66,000,000	13,000,000

Ask the *Maitre d*'s advice. Whatever he says, accuse him of trying to take advantage of both you and your business partner. Tell him you have calculators and you're not afraid to use them.

Second Afternoon Ritual

Office Work Ritual

Go to your place of employment. If you are unemployed, look for a job. If you cannot find a job, go to the public library and pretend you work there.

Take out a copy of the *American Heritage Dictionary*. Pretend to work while actually reading all of the entries for *work*, including the entries for its root, *werg*.

Keep leafing through the dictionary until you hear a colleague sneeze. Offer your colleague the secret rites you've recently learned for curing allergies.

Lie down behind the nearest admin's desk. Tell the admin you are completely drained.

Stay there until the admin threatens to step on you.

Go to the desk or work area of all of your other colleagues. Ask if they would like to stroll with you down the boulevard. Escort any takers down the boulevard.

Produce from your jacket or shirt pocket a harmonica or other miniature organ. Play for spare change in front of your boss's door.

'The rotating shift' may bring to mind a picture of a family carrying on a weekend alone. It can bring to mind a picture of a police family carrying on holiday activities without their police parent. While the officer works a weekend or sleeps after a night shift, the family lives on, together, but apart. Again, the 'job' is central to the lifestyle, central to the image.

The idea of 'rituals' probably doesn't bring a similar image. Most people ***ociate rituals with religious or anti-religious events. However, rituals are one of the most important aspects of a healthy life for a law enforcement family. Rituals are the foundation for a sense of community regardless of whether that community is a congregation, a cult or a family. Webster's dictionary defines a ritual as a pattern of behavior that is repeated in a set manner. If you came from a typical family, you will remember many rituals-- perhaps the evening meal where everyone took turns telling about their day, perhaps Christmas day unwrapping and playing with presents, perhaps something as simple as a nightly story reading and tuck into bed.

Police families often have their rituals interrupted by the demands of the job. Frequently, the officer is not available to participate in the family rituals. When a brick is missing in the foundation, the structure weakens. A weakened structure will more readily feel the damage from a storm. The police family needs to work hard at establishing rituals in order to fortify the normal ups and downs of a marriage. For example, if Dad is an officer and is working a three-to-eleven, he can't be at dinner. The dinner must go on, to steal an old show biz cliche. After everyone tells their story at dinner, the conversation can slip into what to say to Dad when he phones for his evening call. The kids can be given a one or two minute segment of a nightly phone call to present their day to Daddy. This way Daddy becomes part of the dinner, part of the ritual. What's important is that the same pattern is repeated whenever Daddy is on three-to-elevens.

If Mom is an officer and can't be there some nights to tuck in, she can be a topic of discussion at bedtime. "What do you want me to tell Mommy about today? Let's write it down for her. Now give me an extra kiss for Mommy when she comes home." One corrections mom even tapes a nightly message for her kids when she wont be home. It doesn't replace Mommy, but it brings her into the ritual. With a small amount of thought, creativity and a little extra work, the absent partner can always be present in one form or another. The benefits are worth the extra effort. On the job, a partner watches your back, takes care of you. At home, a partner has to do the same. Bring your partner into the rituals. Build the most important foundation of your home, a strong family life.

Third Afternoon Ritual

Outdoor Work Ritual

Go to your place of employment or anywhere you can do manual labor in the presence of others.

Plant three shovels in the earth, side by side, handles sticking straight up.

Surround the shovels with fruit, wine, and tools.

Bring two co-workers or neighbors over to see the shovels.

Get a running start and leap through air, pulling one of the shovels to the ground as you fall.

Invite your co-workers or neighbors to join you.

Ancient Egypt was doubly fortunate, and doubtless owed to this its fabled wealth, in that it possessed two activities, namely, pyramid-building as well as the search for the precious metals, the fruits of which, since they could not serve the needs of man by being consumed, did not stale with abundance. The Middle Ages built cathedrals and sang dirges. Two pyramids, two masses for the dead, are twice as good as one; but not so two railways from London to York.

Fourth Afternoon Ritual

Air Ritual

Go into an open area where you can see the vault of the entire sky. Stay within sight of both a downtown and a wooded area.

Take a deep breath, then dive at the air. Wrestle it to the ground. You will find it easiest to grab by its particulate matter. The oxygen and nitrogen will slide through your fingers and around your wrists like shackles and chains or serpents, so grab the soot quickly.

Once subdued, hold the air aloft for your family to see. Sing a short aria in honor of the air. Hold it close to your chest, near your aorta, and feel for the vibrato of its echo.

Vow that by the wind in your throat you will guard the air as though it were worth more than all your vertebrae.

Place a briar, a worm, a cup of water, and a small fire near a window. Turn the air around to see. Through the window, a meteor shower falls like words onto a page.

March 10, 2003: In a rather slick deal for oil and gas drillers, the U.S. Environmental Protection Agency exempted that industry from a new water regulation aimed at reducing polluted runoff. Under the EPA's phase II stormwater pollution rule, issued during the Clinton administration, construction sites between 1 and 5 acres are now required to obtain a National Pollution Discharge Elimination System (NPDES) permit. But the agency gave the oil and gas industry two years to comply, and will it studies whether a permanent exemption is warranted. Six U.S. Senators promptly fired off a letter to EPA Administrator Christie Todd Whitman, saying there is "voluminous evidence" of an oil and gas industry review before the rule was created in 1999.

Fifth Afternoon Ritual

Boat Ritual

From the only hardware store in the smallest town within 100 miles, buy:

    a. Two short oars
    b. Two life preservers
    c. One outboard motor

From the only marina on the most stump-ridden lake within 100 miles, rent a jon boat.

Drive two children to the middle of the lake, hitting as many stumps on the way as possible, until you break the motor. Repair if possible. Repeat hitting stumps until the motor is completely ruined.

While the wind builds and the storm approaches, fish.

When it begins to rain, row.

Lay the life preservers down for the children to sleep.

At the nearest bank, drag the boat ashore. Lift the motor and wake the children. Move out of the rain and beneath a magnolia.

When the rain stops, walk toward the nearest dirt road.

Before you reach the road, the first child must almost step on a black racer. Let it pass.

Hindu

Manu, the first human, saved a small fish from the jaws of a larger fish. After hearing the smaller one beg for protection, Manu kept the fish safe, transferring it to larger and larger containers as it grew, finally returning it to the ocean.

Because of this kindness, the fish returned to warn Manu about an imminent flood and told him to build a boat, stocking it with samples of every species. After the flood waters rose, Manu tied a rope to the fish's horn. The fish led him to a mountain and told Manu to fasten the ship's rope to a tree so that it would not drift. He stayed on the mountain (known as Manu's Descent) while the flood swept away all living creatures. Manu alone survived.

After you reach the road, the second child must almost step on a coiled copperhead. Throw the motor onto the copperhead. Repeat as necessary to smash both the copperhead and the motor.

Walk until blistered of foot and skin.

At dusk, hitch a ride back to the marina.

Accuse the owner of renting you a leaky boat and endangering the lives of the children. Swear to it. Vow never to return. Swear to it.

Once safely home, provide these directions to the children.

Sixth Afternoon Ritual

Ritual for Doing

Isolate yourself within an arbitrary ring of space.

Have at least one observer, preferably more. Send the observers far enough away that they can only observe with binoculars.

Outline a circle in the air in front of you by passing your hands around it. Move your lips silently as though talking to yourself or praying.

There is no dancing in this ritual, so stop dancing.

With a wave, invite the onlookers to rejoin you. When they arrive, one of them will criticize every move you have made, will say your mystification is reprehensible, that you propagate unhealthy myths, that you are bad for the children.

Refuse to let the critic speak any more by jabbering nonsensically like a child every time he opens his mouth. Invite the others to join you.

There is no dancing in this ritual, so stop dancing.

Draw another circle on the ground. Invite everyone but the critic to stand inside the circle. Move mechanically around the circle, gesturing obscenely at the critic.

Write a profane word on the ground. Spit on it. Erase the word.

Postmodern philosophers and literary theorists in the past two decades have sensitized us to the complications in the search for historical and critical accuracy. (1) Can dance criticism ever "objectively" describe the work? Is there one "correct" description and interpretation of a work? If not, are there limits on the range of acceptable interpretations? Does description necessarily reflect the theoretical, cultural, and personal biases of the critic? Do commentaries upon commentaries only further cloud "the work" as it was perceived by audiences at the time? Can we, today, ever really understand the work as it existed at a moment in time years ago, perceived by observers with different expectations and experiences? Can or should criticism have the status of a work of art itself?

Release the onlookers from their circle and borrow an article of clothing from one of them. Interact with the clothing so that your inner state is revealed by your actions.

There is no dancing in this ritual, so stop dancing.

Seventh Afternoon Ritual

Tree Ritual

Stand.

                                            Anywhere.

Be.

                            Still.

Fifty classes of beings assembled, from myriad bodhisattvas to infinite numbers of bees and insects ... Buddha Sakyamuni lay down on his right side [dying] his head placed in the north and his feet south. His face facing west and his back east, he immediately entered four stages of meditation, and attained *Parinirvana* ... Thereupon, the *arhats*, who were in the state of complete freedom from worldly attachment, forgot their rule of asceticism; bodhisattvas, who were making efforts to reach a higher state of bodhisattvahood, let go their wisom of knowing the brirthlessness of myriad beings. Guhyapada threw away his *vajra* staff and howled into the sky. Great Brahma threw away his net and collapsed on the ground. The king of myriad lions threw himself on the ground and wailed. The water birds, wild geese, and ducks felt deep sorrow. Lion, tiger, boor, and deer all stood hoof-to-hoof, forgetting to attack one another. Gibbons and dogs saddened by grief dropped their heads; ... the great earth shook and quaked; the great mountains collapsed; plants and trees, groves and forest, all cried out their grief.
       - Myoe, Koben (1173-1232), *Rules of Liturgy*

Eighth Afternoon Ritual

Ritual for Eating

Transplant a pecan sapling to your yard. Give it sufficiently rich soil and water.

Transplant a cherry tree to your yard. Place it in sufficient sunlight and give it plenty of water.

Meanwhile, have your guests sit down. As the meal is served, announce that the fruits and nuts will be ready in several years. Invite your guests to take their time with the first few courses.

Shabu Shabu (Boiled Beef)

Shabu-shabu means "swish-swish," referring to the swishing action when you cook a very thin slice of beef in hot water.

On a portable range, place a medium-sized pot (1/2 gallon should do). Place a couple of slices of kombu (a type of kelp) and cover with cold water. Gently bring the water to a boil and remove the kombu just before it actually starts to boil. When the water is boiling very, very gently, you're set.

On your table you should have: (for 4 people)

Ingredients:

1 lb very thinly sliced beef (sirloin), preferably grain-fed.
    Beer-fed Kobe beef is the best. And I mean VERY THIN (less than 1/16 inch)
8 shiitake mushrooms
1/2 lb enoki mushrooms
1/2 lb shimeji mushrooms
1/2 lb shirataki
1 lb chinese cabbage
1/2 lb watercress, to substitute for spring chrysanthemum leaves
1 lb tofu, cut in 1 in. cubes, pressed and drained
any other ingredients you want to use

Dipping sauce:

In a small bowl, you should have 2 parts soy sauce and 1 part lemon juice, as a dipping sauce.

Simply take one of the items, swish it around in the hot water from a few seconds for beef to a few minutes for vegetables. Serve with hot steamed rice.

Copyright (c) Ken Iisaka. May be distributed freely provided this copyright notice is not removed.

Evening Rituals

First Evening Ritual

Negotiation Ritual

Bring the negotiators to a table and seat them across from each other. Do not allow them to speak, eat, or get up for two days.

Light candles in the room and dare the negotiators to swallow one.

Have the negotiators trade sides of the table. Do not let them speak, eat, or get up for three days.

Give the negotiators a brief detente. Feed them grapes. Instruct them to stand and wave their hands over their heads as though flagging down passing motorists for emergency assistance.

Allow each negotiator to kick another negotiator of his or her choice.

Pay each negotiator fifty cents.

Require each negotiator to hold out his or her right hand. Pretend to read their palms, giving particularly grave reports regarding their lifelines.

Inform the negotiators that the negotiations are over, but do not let them leave. Ask them to perform an impromptu skit.

In the middle of the skit, set off a small explosion that destroys one of the chairs and the table.

Light a flare.

Descartes says that the educated often try to demonstrate their intelligence by arguing that what seems to be is not because there is a more fundamental reality.

Descartes also says to think is to be.

Meinong says that it is possible to be without existing.

Meinong also says that the void rises from language; language has the power to create that which is physically impossible.

Some say Descartes and Meinong are both wrong; that it's all in their imaginations.

Second Evening Ritual

Blood Ritual

Under a full moon, a man and a woman must go outside together with a flashlight. The man must open his mouth wide and hold the flashlight up to his cheek until his companion sees the fine, spidery lines inside.

Then she must punch him in the mouth and shake her head at him in disgust until he pulls at his hair in agony.

At midnight, the man must cut his left hand with a piece of plastic. There must be enough blood to cover his palm. He must press his hand against his forehead. Meanwhile, the woman must roll a paper towel into a small cylinder, which he will squeeze in his fist until the bleeding stops.

Then she must take the flashlight and bash him on the forehead, just above the temple. If he does not pass out, she must shine the flashlight to confirm there is blood then decide whether or not to run for safety. If he does pass out, it is up to the woman to decide whether to leave or to wait for him to revive.

When the man is awake and the bleeding has stopped, if the woman is still there, they have intercourse in the open air.

There's nothing in the world a good man would do to deny himself the pleasures of a bad woman he can trust. A good woman will go out of her way for the pleasure of a bad man who won't tell. Not even when the light that is love produces lasting effect. Chastity is a modern form of money, he might say. I must take up arms vigorously, she might say. Annointest me with thine oil. Burn whatever will burn. Slay them all–God will know his own.

Third Evening Ritual

Subatomic Particle Ritual

Dance into a room repeatedly. The first time just peek in the door, and another time come prancing in, waving your arms. Another time stand calmly beneath the lintel and appear to be both in and out of the room. Another time be in the room with only a certain degree of certainty.

Pick a partner and send him/her out of the room. Dance in your separate rooms. Though you cannot see each other, an observer can see that when you spin one way, your partner spins the other. When you spin the other way, your partner changes, too. Surprise your audience by momentarily disappearing, then reappearing in opposite rooms, still spinning.

When the splendor of your dance draws a larger audience, pass through the wall and collide with your partner. Break into a shower of each other, each new self identical to your old selves with one or two strays that spin into oblivion and can hardly be called selves at all. Dance among yourselves a wild dance like Shiva's, sending off sparks and shadows and eating up the floor. Exchange wishes when you tire, and wave as the rest of you fizzles into air.

When the audience turns away, embrace your partner tight. Hold on harder and closer, as close as your skins allow, harder yet until you reach the point where you are in danger of becoming a little sun.

The Simulation

A simulation was designed to test the hypothesis. It models a continuous two-dimensional square area representing a fluid medium. In the model, distances and sizes are measured in abstract world units. The size of the square domain is 6000 by 6000. Nothing can pass beyond its boundary—it is like an aquarium tank.

Organisms in this simulation are called "swimbots", due to a slight machine-like, or *robot*-like appearance. In addition to swimbots, there are food bits, and the medium in which they exist, called, the *fluid*. Time is measured in discrete units of 1, with each time step corresponding to an update of physical forces, swimbot states, and an animation frame. Food is regenerated periodically (one bit every 20 steps) in the fluid, and eaten by swimbots. Swimbots eat, mate, give birth to new swimbots, and die.

Energy

Global energy is set to 150,000 (abstract units), and remains constant. Throughout the simulation it is exchanged between fluid, food, and swimbots, as shown in Figure 1.

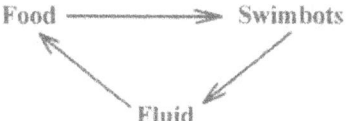

Figure 1. Energy exchange

The fluid contains ambient energy which is gradually converted into new food bits which appear in random locations of the fluid. Each food bit contains 50 units of energy and remains stationary until eaten by a swimbot, which then acquires this energy. Energy is expended in the swimbot from the work of moving body parts. This expended energy is then converted back into ambient energy and stored in the fluid.

FOURTH EVENING RITUAL

Ritual With No Name

Absent Text Regarding the Sound of Your Own Approach

Fifth Evening Ritual

Tree Ritual II

At least one mile from the nearest building, find a mature hardwood.

Invite the tree to your home. If it does not accept, arrange some of your things on the ground: a watch, a pair of shoes, a stack of books, a crystal decanter, a lamp.

Dress the tree in a blouse and a skirt, or a shirt and tie.

Promise the tree that you will reveal this to no one.

Set a dinner table, and finish it off with a pair of iron spikes.

After dinner, sit quietly and listen to the tree.

*[The wind passing through the leaves is yes.
The wind creaking the limbs is no.]*

Johnny Appleseed Crossword Puzzle

Name: _____   Date: _____

ACROSS

2 His friends were the _____.

8 The man who gave away apple seeds was _____.

9 The Indians became his friends when they found him in the forest _____.

12 He was a good _____.

DOWN

1 Johnny Appleseed's real name was John_____

3 When he walked across the U.S. he didn't wear _____.

4 Johnny Appleseed told _____ to the children he visited.

5 Because of Johnny Appleseed, many _____ trees grow in the U.S.

6 The Indians took good ____ of him until he was well again.

7 Johnny Appleseed gave people apple ____ to plant.

10 A drink made from apples is _____.

11 He wore a _____ on his head.

Sixth Evening Ritual

Smoking Ritual

Lay on a table before you a pinecone and a blade of grass. Place a box of refrigerated sand on the floor next to your chair.

Insert as many matches as you can fit into the pinecone, tip out. Light them.

Take off your shoes and put your feet into the box of sand. Wiggle your toes until comfortable.

When the flames reach the pinecone and it begins to singe, lift the blade of grass to your nose and inhale deeply three times. Tell the blade of grass it is lovelier than a dollar bill.

Seventh Evening Ritual

Searchlight Ritual

Just past midnight, open your bedroom window.

Disrobe. Climb out. Walk to the mailbox. Open and shut the mailbox.

Go back inside. Open your living room window. Lean halfway out to see if anyone is watching.

Find the small switch on the front of your spinal column, between your lungs. If someone other than a police officer is watching you, the switch will flip automatically. If a police officer is watching you, close the window and pretend to go to sleep until they leave. If no one is watching you, you must flip the switch yourself. If it helps you to visualize the switch, you may flick your index finger over your solar plexus.

Once the switch is flipped, you will shine with a high-powered beam that rotates out of you, flashing at high speed through the two open windows.

[Whoever is watching may believe they are witness to the birth of a quasar that backlights the skyline and blots out the visible constellations as you...] Move around the house opening windows, shutting windows.

[It is possible you will be unable to see the beam yourself. But when you are still, you will feel it searching.]

"Sir," saith the hermit to Messire Gawain, "The damsel will say her pleasure. May God defend King Arthur, for his father made me knight. Now am I priest, and in this hermitage ever sithence that I came hither have I served King Fisherman by the will of Our Lord and His commandment, and all they that serve him do well partake of his reward, for the place of his most holy service is a refuge so sweet that unto him that hath been there a year, it seemeth to have been but a month for the holiness of the place and of himself, and for the sweetness of his castle wherein have I oftentimes done service in the chapel where the Holy Graal appeareth. Therefore is it that I and all that serve him are so youthful of seeming."

The problems with the Web are many. WWW documents continue to be largely un-attributed, undated, and un-annotated. As a rule, information about the author and publisher is either unavailable or incomplete. Frequently, the rationale for placing a document on line and information about how it relates to other materials is not explicitly stated. It has also been observed that the Web remains a place in which far too many resource catalogues seem to chase far too few original or non-trivial documents and data sets (Ciolek 1995a).

EIGHTH EVENING RITUAL

Numbers Ritual

Throughout your day, recite the names of every age you have been. Count the number of dogs you have owned in that time.

At the first meal, list all of your lovers while counting the number of bites it takes to finish eating.

At the second meal, exclude yourself from all routine. Observe how the world proceeds without you.

At the third meal, take a blood sample. Distinguish between those present and as many of those absent as you can remember during a standing eight-count.

As you drift off in the armchair, recount your most embarrassing moments. Set them adrift in a vessel of your own device, Viking style.

When the lights turn down, count to three and you're off.

```
asciiNumberString = "7654321";
n = asciiNumberString.length - 1;

if ( (n % 2) == 0 ) {   // precondition the number to avoid tests later
   asciiNumberString = '0' + asciiNumberString;
   n++;
}

for ( place = n; place >= 0; place-- ) {
    // initialize and setup our values:
    asciiOne = asciiTen = ethioOne = ethioTen = '';

    asciiOne = asciiNumberString[n - place];
    place--;
    asciiTen = asciiNumberString[n - place];

    if ( asciiOne != '0' )
       ethioOne = asciiOne + ('፩' - '1');   // map onto Ethiopic "ones"

    if ( asciiTen != '0' )
       ethioTen = asciiTen + ('፲' - '1');   // map onto Ethiopic "tens"

    pos = ( place % 4 ) / 2;   // ፼ for even subscripts, ፻ for odd

    // find a separator, if any, to follow ethioTen and ethioOne:
    sep = ( place != 0 )
           ? ( pos != 0 )
               ? ( ( ethioOne != '' ) || ( ethioTen != '' ) )
                   ? '፻'
                   : ''
               : '፼'
           : '';

    // remove '፩' under special conditions:
    if ( ( ethioOne == '፩' ) && ( ethioTen != '' ) && ( n > 1 ) ) {
         if ( ( sep == '፻' ) || ( (place+1) == n ) )
            ethioOne = '';
    }

    //  append the result
    ethioNumberString += ethioTen + ethioOne + sep;
}

return( ethioNumberString );
```

Notes & Sources

Rituals open on the verso, with a corresponding text (and/or image) on the recto. Longer rituals continue on the following verso.

First Morning Ritual: Daniel B. Lee, quoted from his paper, "On the Social Meaning and Meaninglessness of Religion," found at http://www.performativ.de/en/beliefs-religion-rituals.html

Second Morning Ritual: Dante Alighieri, *La Vita Nuova*, translated by A.S. Kline, found at http://www.poetryintranslation.com/klineasthenewlife.htm

Third Morning Ritual: Top, Coffee Beans, "History of Coffee," from http://www.coffeebeans.ie/about-coffee-page34053.html; Bottom, "Did You Know?" from http://www.delanceystreetbagels.com/coffeelb.php. The text regarding the Boston Tea Party and coffee is widely cited, especially on social media for coffee companies, in this and other close variations. The original source is unknown.

Fourth Morning Ritual: Charles Darwin, *The Origin of Species*

Fifth Morning Ritual: Su Shi, "The Red Cliff," from http://afe.easia.columbia.edu/ps/china/sushi_redcliff.pdf

Sixth Morning Ritual: Robert Temple, *The Sirius Mystery*, from http://www.godsebook.org/Robert_Temple_-_The_Sirius_Mystery.pdf

Eighth Morning Ritual: Walt Whitman, "The Wound Dresser," from http://www.poetryfoundation.org/poem/237970

First Afternoon Ritual: Top, Dinesh D'Souza, "Two Cheers for Colonialism," originally published in *The Chronicle of Higher Education*, May 10, 2002, from http://www.sfgate.com/opinion/article/Two-cheers-for-colonialism-2799327.php; Bottom, Mary Evelyn Townsend, *European Colonial Expansion Since 1871* (Chicago: J.P. Lippincott Company, 1941), p. 19

Second Afternoon Ritual: National Police Wives Association, from http://www.policewivesonline.org/community/showthread.php?t=14

Third Afternoon Ritual: John Maynard Keynes, *The General Theory of Employment, Interest and Money*

Fourth Afternoon Ritual: Natural Resources Defense Council, post on 6/25/2010, at http://www.2ndlight.com/fusetalk/forum/ textthread.cfm?catid=4&threadid=110168&filtmsgid=1042661

Fifth Afternoon Ritual: Hindu flood myth, from http://www.dreamscape.com/morgana/titania.htm

Sixth Afternoon Ritual: Julie Van Camp, "Dance Criticism by Croce, Denby, and Siegel," *Dance Research Journal,* Vo. 24, No. 2 (Fall 1992): 41-44, from http://www.csulb.edu/~jvancamp/article6.html

Seventh Afternoon Ritual: Top, Ito Jakuchu (1716-1800), *Yasai Nehan (Vegetable Nirvana);* Bottom, Myoe, Koben (1173-1232), *Rules of Liturgy*; both from http://www.gardendigest.com/zen/vegnir.htm

Eighth Afternoon Ritual: recipe by Ken Iisaka, from http://www.globalgourmet.com/destinations/japan/shabushabu.html#axzz3C543xOWU

Third Evening Ritual: Jeffrey Ventrella, "Attractiveness vs. Efficiency: How Mate Preference Affects Locomotion in the Evolution of Artificial Swimming Organisms," *Artificial Life VI,* 1998, MIT Press.

Fifth Evening Ritual: "Johnny Appleseed Crossword Puzzle," Marshall Elementary School, Lewisburg, Tenn., from http://mupfc.marshall.edu/~jones366/worksheet4.pdf

Sixth Evening Ritual: image from http://www.erowid.org/plants/show_image.php?i=cannabis/images/archive/marijuana_propaganda_poster2.gif

Seventh Evening Ritual: Top, "The High History of the Holy Graal, Branch III," from http://www.sacred-texts.com/neu/graal/branch03.htm; Bottom, T. Matthew Ciolek, "The Six Quests for The Electronic Grail: Current Approaches to Information Quality in WWW Resources," Coombs Computing Unit, Research School of Social Sciences, Australian National University, 6/20/1996

Eighth Evening Ritual: Open source code (in C) for a bug fix for converting Arabic numerals to Ethiopic, from http://www.ethiopic.org/Numerals/

quale [kwa-lay]: *Eng.* n 1. A property (such as hardness) considered apart from things that have that property. 2. A property that is experienced as distinct from any source it may have in a physical object. *Ital.* pron.a. 1. Which, what. 2. Who. 3. Some. 4. As, just as.

www.ingramcontent.com/pod-product-compliance
Lightning Source LLC
Chambersburg PA
CBHW021024090426
42738CB00007B/897